ESSENTIAL ELEMENTS

FOR STRINGS

A COMPREHENSIVE STRING METHOD

By
Michael Allen • Robert Gillespie • Pamela Tellejohn Hayes
Arrangements by John Higgins

CONGRATULATIONS and WELCOME to Book 2 of Essential Elements for Strings!

By now you are well aware of the benefits and joy of playing the double bass in the orchestra. Book 2 will help you to reach a more advanced level, and your musical experiences will become even more fun and exciting.

But remember, all of the techniques you learned and practiced in Book 1, especially instrument position, left hand shape, and fingerings and bowings, are even more important now. These skills need to be refined, and in order to progress, you must continue to practice carefully and regularly.

There will be rewards for your effort! As you spend time learning more challenging material, the mastery of new skills will bring you even more joy in the years to come. Good luck and best wishes for a lifetime of musical happiness!

ISBN 0-7935-4300-2

HAL•LEONARD™
CORPORATION
7777 W. BLUEMOUND RD. P.O. BOX 13819 MILWAUKEE, WI 53213

00862552

Theory **Major Scale** A Major Scale is a series of eight notes that follow a definite pattern of whole steps and half steps. Half steps appear only between scale steps 3-4 and 7-8. Every major scale has the same arrangement of whole steps and half steps.

1. D MAJOR SCALE - Round

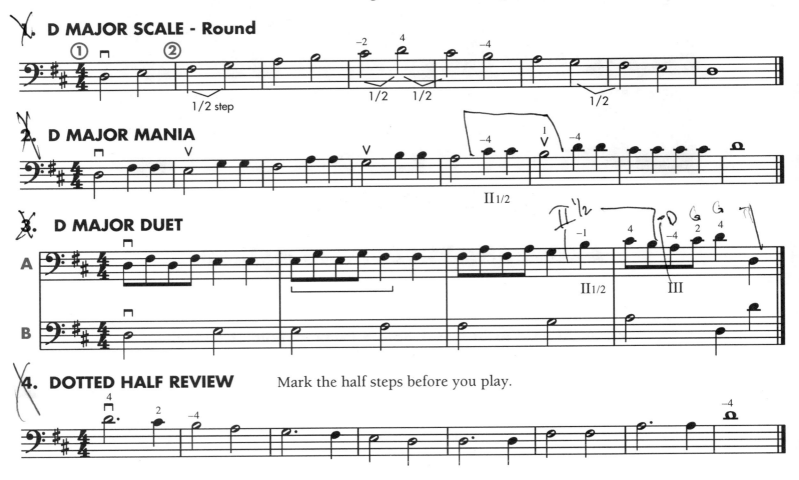

2. D MAJOR MANIA

3. D MAJOR DUET

4. DOTTED HALF REVIEW   Mark the half steps before you play.

Theory **Interval** The distance between two notes is called an interval. Start with "1" on the lower note, and count each line and space between the notes. The number of the higher note is the distance, or name, of the interval.

5. SCALE INTERVALS

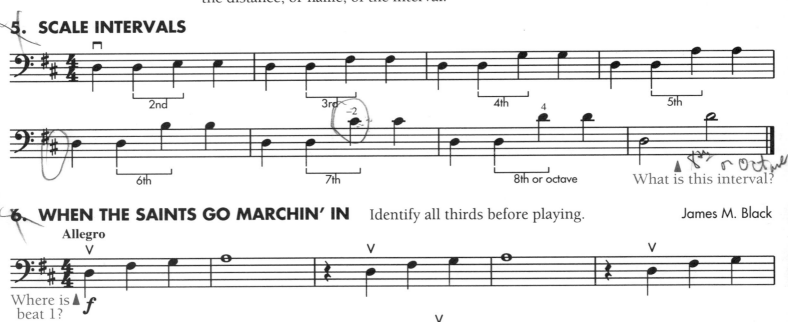

What is this interval?

6. WHEN THE SAINTS GO MARCHIN' IN   Identify all thirds before playing.

James M. Black

Allegro

Where is beat 1?

4

12. C MAJOR SCALE - Round

13. UPPER LEVEL Remember to count.

Slur 4 notes.

1 & 2 &   1 & 2 &   1 & 2 &   1 & 2 &   1 & 2 &   1 & 2 &   1 & 2 &   1 & 2 &

14. C MAJOR ARPEGGIOS - Duet

Intonation How well each note is played in tune.

15. INTONATION ENCOUNTER - Duet

Dynamics *mp* (mezzo piano) Play moderately soft.
mf (mezzo forte) Play moderately loud.

p piano
mp mezzo piano
mf mezzo forte
f forte

16. ESSENTIAL ELEMENTS QUIZ - BUFFALO GALS

John Hodges

Allegro

17. SALSA SIESTA - Duet

Allegretto ◄ A lively tempo, faster than *Andante*, but slower than *Allegro*.

Work-outs

Hand position – Shifting & vibrato –

Tunneling
Slide your fingers up and down the fingerboard between 2 strings.

Ridin' The Rails
Slide up and down one string with your fingers.

Tappin' And Slidin'
Tap your fingers on any string, slide toward the other end of the fingerboard, and tap again.

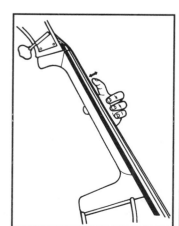
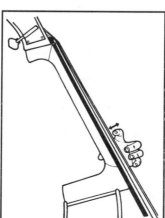

History Jesse James (1847-1882) was an outlaw and gunslinger. He made his living by robbing banks and trains throughout Missouri and Kansas. No. 26. *Jesse James* is an American folk song about this Robin Hood legend who helped the poor. During his lifetime, French impressionistic painters Edouard Manet and Claude Monet created some of their most famous paintings, author Herman Melville wrote *Moby Dick*, and Lewis Carroll wrote *Alice in Wonderland*.

26. ESSENTIAL ELEMENTS QUIZ - JESSE JAMES

American Folk Song

Sightreading Playing a musical selection for the first time is called sightreading. The key to sightreading success is to know what to look for before playing the piece. Follow the guidelines below, and your orchestra will be sightreading STARS! Use the word **STARS** to remind yourself what to look for before reading a selection the first time.

S — **Sharps or flats** in the **key signature**   Identify the key signature first. Silently practice notes from the key signature. Look for key signature changes in the piece.

T — **Time signature** and **tempo markings**   Identify and look for changes in the piece.

A — **Accidentals**   Check for any sharps, flats, or naturals not found in the key signature.

R — **Rhythm**   Slowly count and shadow bow all difficult rhythms. Pay special attention to rests.

S — **Signs**   Look for all signs that indicate bowings, dynamics, tempo changes, repeats, 1st and 2nd endings, and any other instructions printed on your music.

27. SIGHTREADING CHALLENGE #1   Remember to count.

28. SIGHTREADING CHALLENGE #2

29. SIGHTREADING CHALLENGE #3

Review Work-outs on page 5 daily.

8

Dotted Quarter Note
Eighth Note

 = 2 Beats

Remember, a dot adds half the value of the note.

Remember, a single eighth note has a flag on the stem.

 Flag

30. RHYTHM RAP

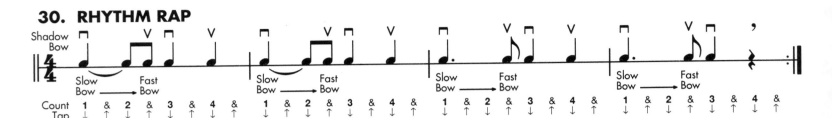

31. THE DOT ALWAYS COUNTS

Fermata 🠒 Hold the note longer.

32. G MAJOR BONANZA - Duet

33. RHYTHM RAP

34. C MAJOR SEQUENCE

Chorales are German hymns or songs that were first written by **Martin Luther** (1483-1546) to help people sing together during church services. While Luther was writing his chorales, Michelangelo began painting the ceiling in the Sistine Chapel in Rome (1508), and Ponce de Leon discovered Florida (1513). The *St. Anthony Chorale* is attributed to the great Austrian composer **Franz Joseph Haydn** (1732-1809).

Legato Play in a smooth and connected style.

40. SMOOTH CONNECTIONS

1 & 2 & 3 & 1 & 2 & 3 & 1 & 2 & 3 & 1 & 2 & 3 & 1 & 2 & 3 & 1 & 2 & 3 & 1 & 2 & 3 & 1 & 2 & 3 &

41. WATCH THE DOT

Fast Slow
Bow Bow——→   Fast Slow
Bow Bow——→

e = The Italian word for "and".

42. LULLABY

Johannes Brahms

Early **Korean music** was influenced by the music of China, but eventually developed its own special style, often using native Korean folk songs. The first Korean music was performed in the courts of Korea's rulers by orchestras with exotic string instruments like the *haekeum*, *komungo*, and the *kayakeum* - an instrument which had 12 bridges!

43. ARIRANG

Korean Folk Song

44. SIGHTREADING CHALLENGE #4   Review the **STARS** guidelines before sightreading (p.7).

45. SIGHTREADING CHALLENGE #5

Theory **Key Change** Sometimes a key signature will change in the middle of a piece of music. You will usually see a thin double bar line at a key change. Keep going, making sure you are playing all the correct notes in the new signature.

46. WHERE, OH WHERE IS MY KEY?

47. AMERICA THE BEAUTIFUL - Orchestra Arrangement

Samuel Augustus Ward
Arr. John Higgins

A = Melody. **B** = Harmony. For orchestral playing, the basses play part B.

Continue reviewing Work-outs on page 5.

Bb (B-FLAT) IN HALF POSITION

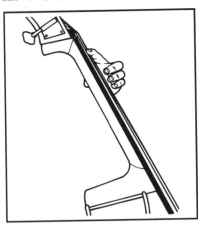

Bb

is played with 1 finger on the A string in half position (1/2).

Listening Skills Play what your teacher plays. Listen carefully.

48. LET'S READ "Bb" (B-flat)

Play with 4 fingers in half position.

49. VIKING WAY

1/2 Notice the fingerings when in half position.

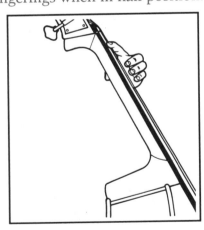

F

is played with 1 finger on the E string in half position (1/2).

50. CAVALIER COUNTRY

▲ Play with 4 fingers in half position.

51. F MAJOR SCALE   F MAJOR Key Signature

Play all B's as Bb (B-flat).

A **Concerto** is a composition in several movements for solo instrument and orchestra. No. 52. *Theme from Violin Concerto* is from the first movement of *Violin Concerto* for violin and orchestra by **Ludwig van Beethoven** (1770-1827), composed while author William Wordsworth was creating some of his works. A special feature of the concerto is the *cadenza*, a section of the concerto that is improvised, or made up, by the soloist during a concert. Improvising and creating your own music is great fun. Jazz players do it all the time. Try it if you have not already.

52. THEME FROM VIOLIN CONCERTO

Ludwig van Beethoven

53. ECHO-LOGICAL   Remember to count.

54. ESSENTIAL ELEMENTS QUIZ - A CAPITAL SHIP

American Folk Song

55. SIGHTREADING CHALLENGE #6   Review the **STARS** guidelines before sightreading.

56. SIGHTREADING CHALLENGE #7

B♭

is played with 2 fingers on the G string in first position (I).

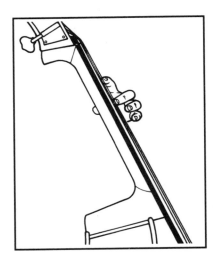

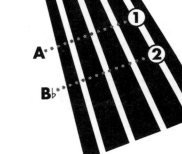

Listening Skills Play what your teacher plays. Listen carefully.

57. LET'S READ "B♭" (B-flat)

58. ROLLING ALONG

Moderato

59. MATCHING OCTAVES

60. TRUMPET VOLUNTARY IN F

Henry Purcell

Andantino

SPECIAL DOUBLE BASS EXERCISE

While the violins are learning a new note, choose any one note on the staff and make up a rhythm exercise. Use each of the following notes and rests at least once (♩. ♩ ♩ ♪ ▬ 𝄽 ♩). Be sure to line up your notes and rests with the counting. After you finish, shadow bow the exercise.

1 & 2 & 3 & 4 &   1 & 2 & 3 & 4 &   1 & 2 & 3 & 4 &   1 & 2 & 3 & 4 &

Listening Skills   Play what your teacher plays. Listen carefully.

61. LET'S READ "F" (F-natural) - Review

62. TECHNIQUE TRAX

63. F MAJOR SCALE   Remember to count.

64. MORE TECHNIQUE TRAX

65. THIRDS IN F MAJOR

66. SILVER MOON

Chinese Folk Song

67. ESSENTIAL ELEMENTS QUIZ - AMERICAN PATROL

F.W. Meacham

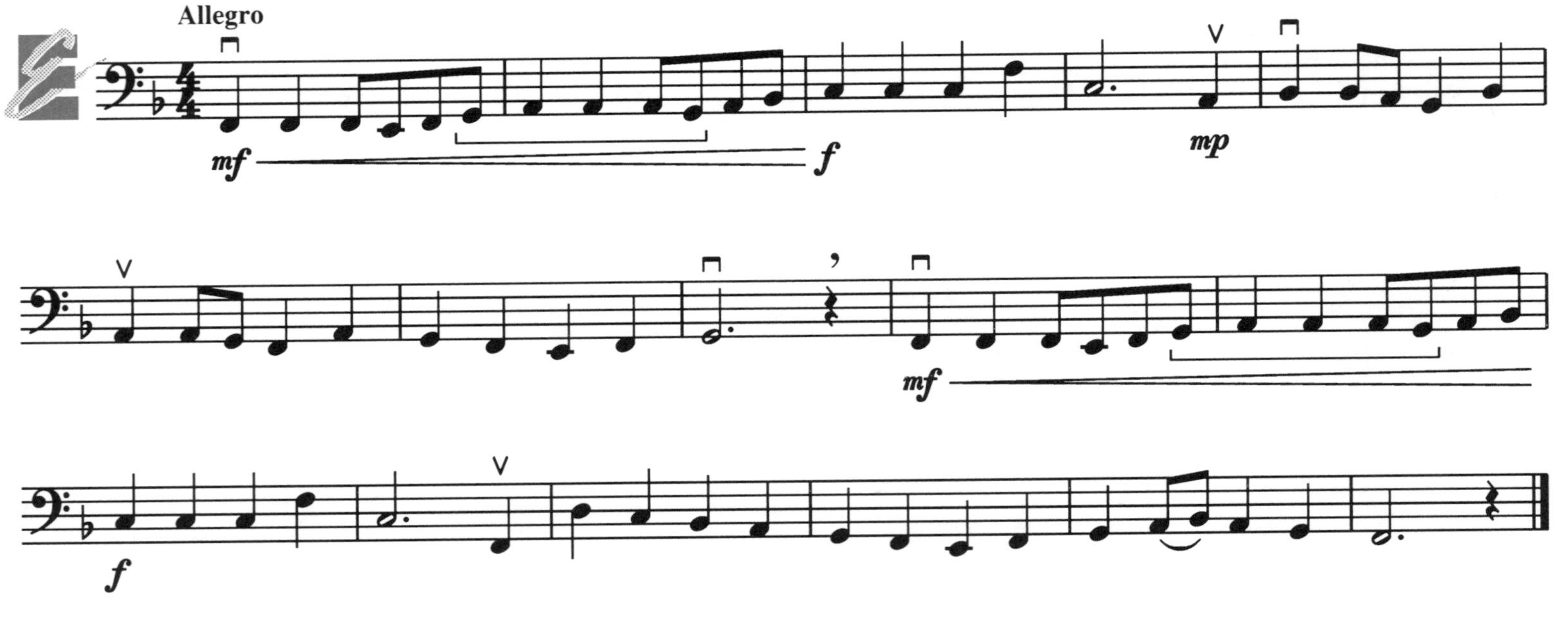

Theory **Minor Scales** A **minor scale** is a series of eight notes which follow a definite pattern of whole steps and half steps. The three forms of the minor scale are natural minor, harmonic minor, and melodic minor. The D minor (*natural*) scale uses the same pitches as the F major scale.

68. D MINOR (Natural) SCALE

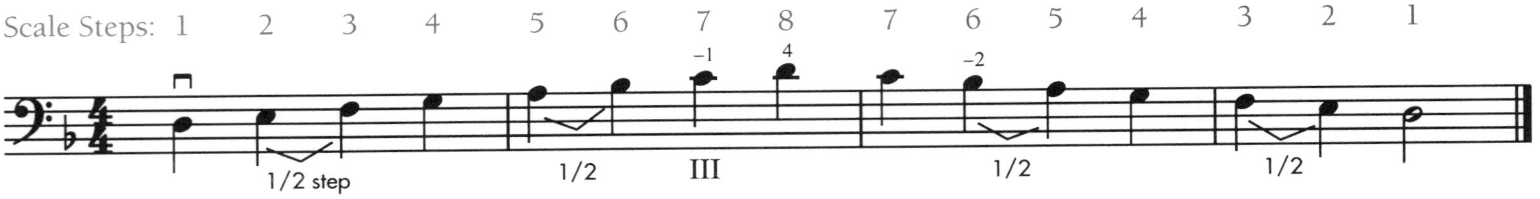

History German composer **Gustav Mahler** (1860-1911) was also a successful conductor. He believed in unifying the arts and often combined music, poetry, and philosophy in his compositions. No. 69. *Mahler's Theme* first appears in his *Symphony No. 1*, played as a solo by the double bass. During Mahler's lifetime Vincent van Gogh created his most famous paintings, and Mark Twain wrote *Tom Sawyer*.

69. MAHLER'S THEME - Round

Gustav Mahler

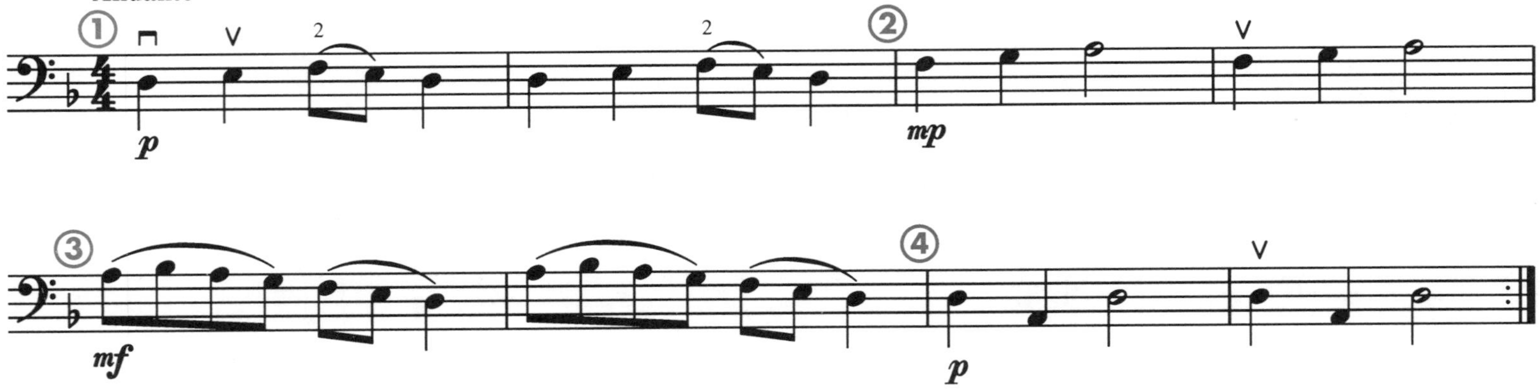

70. SHALOM CHAVERIM

Hebrew Folk Song

71. HOME ON THE RANGE

Dr. Brewster Higley
Daniel E. Kelley

Gustav Holst (1874-1934) was a famous British orchestra composer who frequently set words to music, including poems by the American poet, Walt Whitman. Holst's *St. Paul's Suite* for string orchestra was written for the St. Paul's Girls School Orchestra and published in 1913. His best known work is *The Planets*, first performed in 1918, the same year as the end of World War I.

72. IN THE BLEAK MIDWINTER - Orchestra Arrangement

Gustav Holst
Arr. John Higgins

Team Work Great musicians give encouragement to their fellow performers. Violin, viola, and cello players will now learn a new challenging skill. The success of your orchestra depends on everyone's talent and patience. Play your best as members of these sections advance their musical technique.

SPECIAL DOUBLE BASS EXERCISE

Draw a note next to each printed note that will match the interval number shown. The note you draw can be higher or lower than the printed note. The first one is done for you.

(Example)
2nd   5th   3rd   (go lower only) octave   4th   (go lower only) 6th   (go lower only) 7th

Listening Skills   Play what your teacher plays. Listen carefully.

73. LET'S READ "C#" (C-sharp) - Review

74. AT PIERROT'S DOOR

Andante

75. STAY SHARP

76. HOT CROSS BUNS

Moderato

G♯ (G-SHARP) IN HALF POSITION

G♯

is played with 1 finger on the G string in half position (1/2).

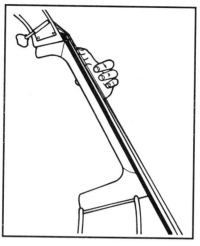

Listening Skills Play what your teacher plays. Listen carefully.

77. LET'S READ "G♯" (G-sharp)

78. REACHING OUT

Play with 2 fingers in half position.

79. HIGHER AND HIGHER

80. A MAJOR SCALE

A MAJOR Key Signature

Play all F's as **F♯** (F-sharp), C's as **C♯** (C-sharp), and G's as **G♯** (G-sharp).

81. AYN KAYLOKAYNU

Return to original tempo. ▼   Traditional Jewish Song

Andantino

A Tempo

20

 **Meter Change** Occasionally the meter (time signature) changes in music. Watch for meter changes and count carefully.

82. RHYTHM RAP

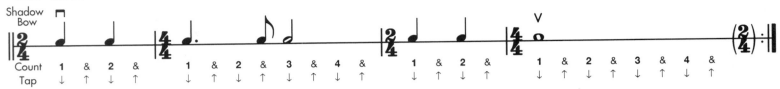

83. KUM BA YAH   Remember to count.

African Spiritual

84. FRENCH FOLK SONG

85. SWEET BETSY FROM PIKE

North American Folk Song

G#

is played with 4 fingers on the E string in first position (I).

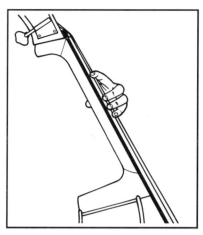

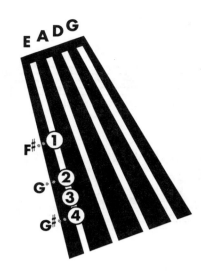

Listening Skills   Play what your teacher plays. Listen carefully.

91. LET'S READ "G#" (G-sharp)

92. A MAJOR SCALE

Cantabile   In a singing style.

93. DUTCH CHORALE

94. SITKA CITY   Remember to count.

Russian Folk Song

95. ESSENTIAL ELEMENTS QUIZ - THE FIG TREE

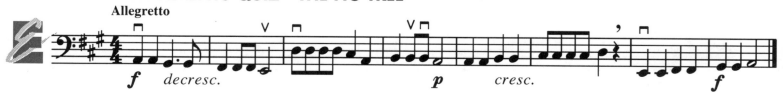

96. LAS MAÑANITAS

Mexican Folk Song

97. ARKANSAS TRAVELER - Orchestra Arrangement

American Folk Song
Arr. John Higgins

Continue reviewing Work-outs on page 5.

24

Listening Skills Play what your teacher plays. Listen carefully.

98. LET'S READ "F#" (F-sharp) - Review

99. HIGH POINT

100. MAGNIFICENT MONTANA

101. D MAJOR SCALE

History **Cantatas** are pieces much like short operas that were written during the Baroque Period (1600-1750). They involve vocal soloists and choirs that are accompanied by small orchestras. **Johann Sebastian Bach** (1685-1750) is considered the master of the cantata, and he wrote nearly 300 of them between 1704 and 1745. His "Peasant Cantata" was composed in 1742 when he was living in Leipzig, Germany. While Bach was composing his cantatas, the famous philosopher Voltaire was writing his books and Thomas Jefferson, the great United States president, was born.

102. MARCH FROM PEASANT'S CANTATA

Johann Sebastian Bach

103. ODE TO JOY

Ludwig van Beethoven

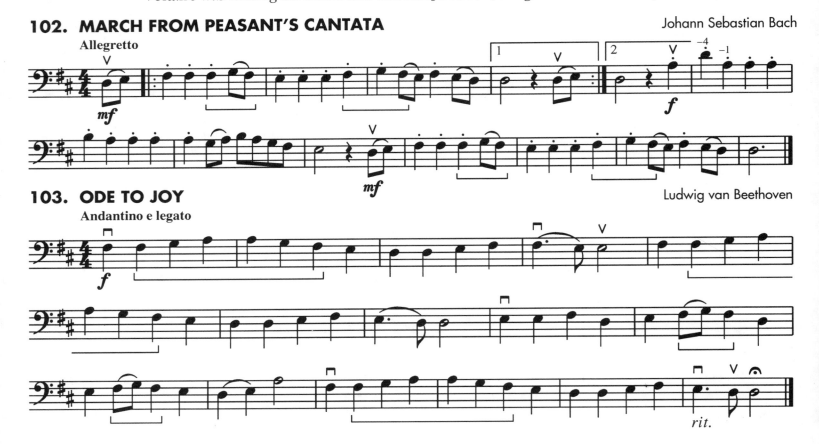

In the second half of the 1800s many composers tried to express the spirit of their own country by writing music with a distinct national flavor. Listen to the music of Scandinavian and Spanish composers, and Russians such as Borodin, Tchaikovsky and Rimsky-Korsakov. They often used folk songs and dance rhythms to convey their nationalism.

104. RUSSIAN FOLK TUNE

E is played with 4 fingers on the G string in fourth position (IV).

D is played with 1 finger on the G string in fourth position (IV).

Note: The entire fingerboard is not shown, as indicated by the break. Use third position as a guide to find fourth position.

105. BOTANY BAY   Remember to count.

Australian Folk Song

106. ESSENTIAL ELEMENTS QUIZ - ALL THROUGH THE NIGHT

Traditional Welsh Air

Do not repeat on the D.C.

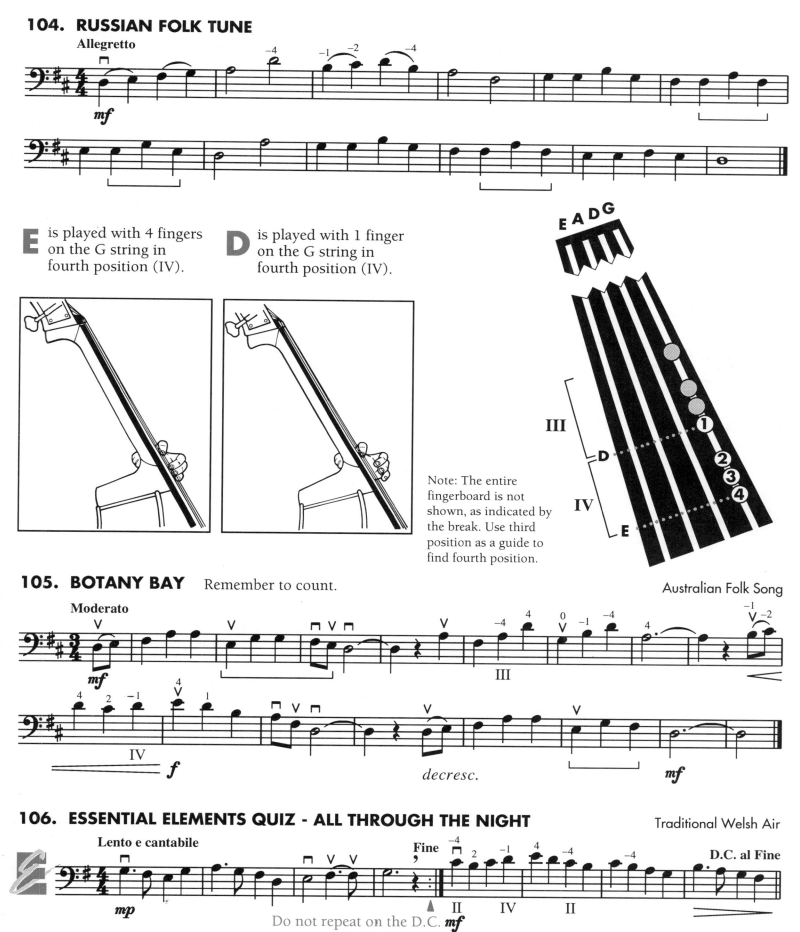

Sixteenth Notes   4 sixteenth notes = 1 beat

A single sixteenth note has 2 flags on the stem.

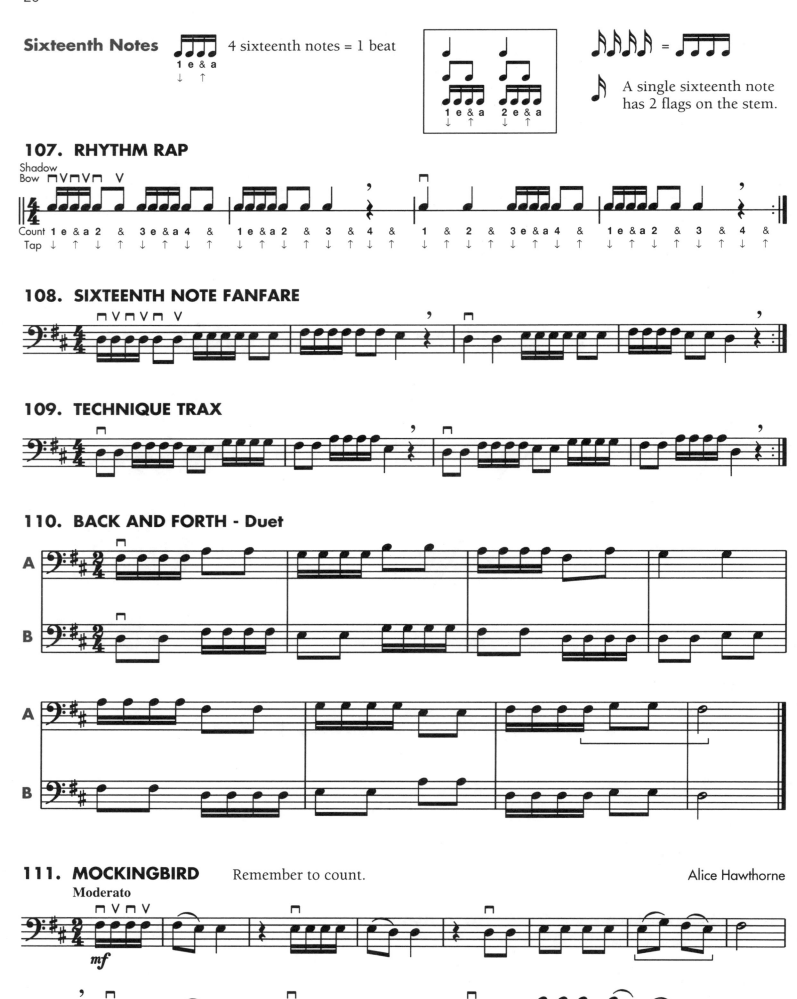

107. RHYTHM RAP

108. SIXTEENTH NOTE FANFARE

109. TECHNIQUE TRAX

110. BACK AND FORTH - Duet

111. MOCKINGBIRD   Remember to count.   Alice Hawthorne

Moderato

mf

112. RHYTHM RAP

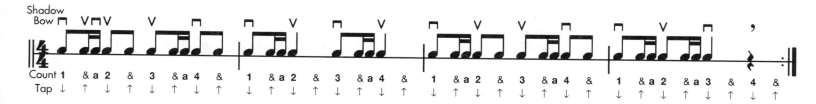

113. BLUEBERRY PIE

114. TECHNIQUE TRAX

115. RHYTHM RAP

116. MARCHING ALONG

117. ON THE MOVE

118. RHYTHM ETUDE - Duet

119. ESSENTIAL ELEMENTS QUIZ - RHYTHM ROUND-UP

Henry Purcell (1659-1695) was a singer and organist who became one of the most famous composers in the 17th century in England. He composed music for many plays that were performed in schools throughout England, including his famous opera *Dido and Aeneas* in 1689. While Purcell was composing his music in England, New Amsterdam became New York (1664), and Philadelphia was founded by William Penn (1682).

126. TRUMPET TUNE

Henry Purcell

127. HOOKED ON D MINOR (Natural)

128. ESSENTIAL ELEMENTS QUIZ - THE SAILOR

Traditional Sea Chantey

 **Syncopation**

In many types of music, the emphasis occurs on notes that do not normally receive a strong pulse or beat. This is called **syncopation** and is very common in jazz, rock, and pop, as well as in classical music.

129. RHYTHM RAP

130. SYNCOPATION TIME

131. CHILDREN'S SHOES

Black American Spiritual

132. HOOKED ON SYNCOPATION

133. TOM DOOLEY

American Folk Song

134. SLOVAKIAN FOLK SONG

135. ESSENTIAL ELEMENTS QUIZ - LUCKY LARRY

136. SIGHTREADING CHALLENGE #11   Review the **STARS** guidelines before sightreading.

137. SIGHTREADING CHALLENGE #12

138. POMP AND CIRCUMSTANCE - Orchestra Arrangement

Edward Elgar
Arr. John Higgins

▲ Play with 2 fingers in half position.

32

E♭ (E-FLAT) IN HALF POSITION

E♭ is played with 1 finger on the D string in half position (1/2).

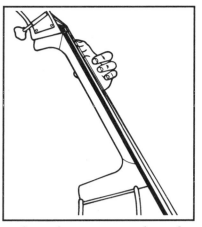

Listening Skills Play what your teacher plays. Listen carefully.

139. LET'S READ "E♭" (E-flat)

140. UP AND DOWN

141. HIKING ALONG

1/2 ▲ Play with 4 fingers in half position.

142. B♭ MAJOR SCALE — B♭ MAJOR Key Signature

Play all B's as **B♭** (B-flat) and all E's as **E♭** (E-flat).

143. THE RAKES OF MALLOW

Irish Folk Song

Henry Carey (1689-1743) was an English dramatist, poet, and composer. No. 144. *America* is based upon his melody "God Save The Queen", which became popular in the 1790s in England because of the British king's ill health and the Napoleonic wars. The year Carey died, Thomas Jefferson was born and Voltaire wrote *Mérope*.

144. AMERICA

Henry Carey

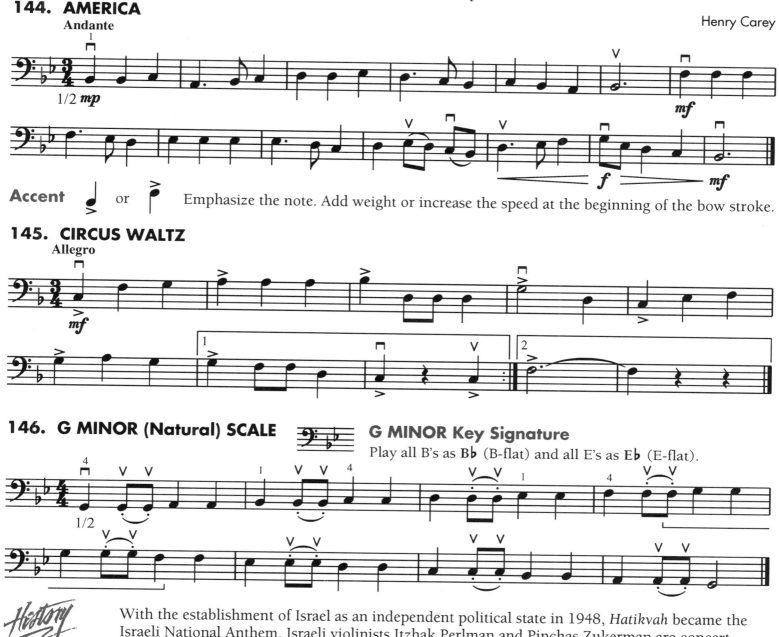

Accent ♩ or ♩ Emphasize the note. Add weight or increase the speed at the beginning of the bow stroke.

145. CIRCUS WALTZ

146. G MINOR (Natural) SCALE

G MINOR Key Signature
Play all B's as **B♭** (B-flat) and all E's as **E♭** (E-flat).

With the establishment of Israel as an independent political state in 1948, *Hatikvah* became the Israeli National Anthem. Israeli violinists Itzhak Perlman and Pinchas Zukerman are concert artists known throughout the world. The same year Israel became a state, Mohandas Gandhi was assassinated in India.

147. ESSENTIAL ELEMENTS QUIZ - HATIKVAH

Israeli National Anthem

SPECIAL DOUBLE BASS EXERCISE

While the violins and violas are learning new notes, match the following words with the correct definitions. Write the correct letter of the definition in the blank next to the words.

1. _____ Allegretto
2. _____ Sixteenth Notes
3. _____ Cantabile
4. _____ Henry Purcell
5. _____ Decrescendo
6. _____ Gustav Mahler
7. _____ e
8. _____ Legato
9. _____ Franz Joseph Haydn
10. _____ Chorale
11. _____ Intonation
12. _____ Lento
13. _____ Fermata
14. _____ mezzo forte
15. _____ Dotted Quarter Note
16. _____ Ritardando
17. _____ Concerto
18. _____ Syncopation
19. _____ Andantino
20. _____ Accent

a. German hymn or song.
b. How well each note is played in tune.
c. Austrian composer.
d. Play in a smooth and connected style.
e. Hold the note longer.
f. A very slow tempo.
g. One and one-half beats of sound.
h. German composer.
i. The Italian word for "and".
j. Play moderately loud.
k. Gradually decrease volume.
l. English composer.
m. In a singing style.
n. Gradually slow the tempo.
o. A tempo that is slightly quicker than Andante.
p. Four of these = One beat of sound.
q. A lively tempo.
r. Emphasize the note.
s. Emphasis on the weak beats of the music.
t. A composition in several movements for solo instrument and orchestra.

Listening Skills Play what your teacher plays. Listen carefully.

148. LET'S READ "E♭" (E-flat) - Review

149. LET'S READ "B♭" (B-flat) - Review

150. B♭ MAJOR SCALE - Review

151. REACHING HIGHER Remember to count.

Team Work Great musicians give encouragement to their fellow performers. Viola and cello players will now learn a new challenging skill. The success of your orchestra depends on everyone's talent and patience. Play your best as members of these sections advance their musical technique.

Listening Skills Play what your teacher plays. Listen carefully.

152. LET'S READ "E♭" (E-flat) - Review

153. MOVING ALONG

154. BELLS OF BLUE

155. SAKURA, SAKURA

Japanese Folk Song

36

162. ESSENTIAL ELEMENTS QUIZ - TO A WILD ROSE

Edward MacDowell

163. RHYTHM RAP

164. DOWN HOME

165. COUNTRY JAM - Orchestra Arrangement

John Higgins

38

Time Signature (Meter) $\frac{6}{8}$ - 6 beats per measure - ♪ or 𝄾 gets one beat (slower music)

♪	= 1 beat
♩	= 2 beats
♩.	= 3 beats
♩. (dotted half)	= 6 beats

When music is slow, $\frac{6}{8}$ time should be counted 6 beats to a measure with the eighth note receiving 1 beat. Place a slight accent on beats 1 and 4 when tapping and counting aloud.

Conducting

Practice conducting this six-beat pattern.

166. RHYTHM RAP

167. LAZY DAY

168. COASTING ALONG

169. ROW, ROW, ROW YOUR BOAT - Round

Time Signature (Meter) $\frac{6}{8}$ - 2 beats per measure - ♩. or 𝄾. gets one beat (faster music)

♪	= 1/3 beat
♩	= 2/3 beat
♩.	= 1 beat
♩. (dotted half)	= 2 beats

When music is fast, $\frac{6}{8}$ time should be counted 2 beats to a measure with 3 eighth notes (or their equivalent) receiving one beat.

170. RHYTHM RAP

171. RISE AND FALL

172. JOLLY GOOD FELLOW

Andante

173. WHEN JOHNNY COMES MARCHING HOME

Remember to count.

Patrick Gilmore

Allegretto

174. ESSENTIAL ELEMENTS QUIZ - OVER THE RIVER

Moderato

175. SIGHTREADING CHALLENGE #13

Review the **STARS** guidelines before sightreading.

Moderato

Triplets A triplet is a group of three notes. In 2/4, 3/4, or 4/4 time, an eighth note triplet is played in one beat.

176. RHYTHM RAP

177. TRIPLET TUNE

178. G MAJOR SCALE WITH TRIPLETS

179. THEME FROM FAUST

Charles Gounod

Moderato

180. MARCH FROM THE NUTCRACKER - Duet

Tchaikovsky

Allegretto

Double Stops Playing two strings at once.

181. TWO AT A TIME

182. DOUBLE DUTY

183. ADDING FINGERS

184. TRICKY TUNNELS

Bariolage A bowing style where no two notes in a row are played on the same string. This can involve two, three, or four strings. Practice the following two lines slowly with single bows. Then try adding two and four note slurs.

185. STRING CROSSING

186. CROSS OVER AGAIN

Improvisation The art of performing music freely, creating your own melody as you play.

187. YOU NAME IT

Make up your own melody to go with the accompaniment line.
Don't write it in, so that you can play a different melody next time.

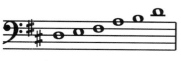

Use these notes to make up a melody. Accompaniment

INTRODUCING FIFTH AND A HALF POSITION AND HARMONICS

Shape your hand on the G string as shown, for fifth and a half position (V1/2).

When playing the harmonic G, lightly touch the G string with your 3rd finger.

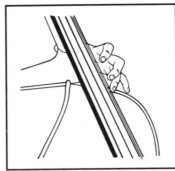

Note: The entire fingerboard is not shown, as indicated by the break. Use fourth position as a guide to find fifth and a half position.

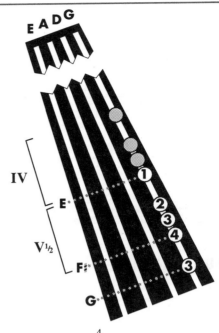

Listening Skills Play what your teacher plays. Listen carefully.

188. NEW POSITION (for violins and violas)

189. SMOOTH SAILING

190. STARTING HIGHER

New notes: F#

191. OZARK CROSSING

192. SUMMER SUNRISE

193. IN REVERSE

194. A SONG FOR ANNE

Moderato

mf

Team Work Great musicians give encouragement to their fellow performers. Violin players will now learn a new challenging skill. The success of your orchestra depends on everyone's talent and patience. Play your best as members of this section advance their musical technique.

 Play what your teacher plays. Listen carefully.

195. STILL HIGHER

196. D MAJOR SCALE

197. SKY HIGH

198. TRYING IT OUT

199. SHIFT AGAIN Remember to count.

200. TWO TO ONE

45

209. F MAJOR SCALE AND ARPEGGIO

210. Bb MAJOR SCALE AND ARPEGGIO (Upper Octave - Violin)

211. Bb MAJOR SCALE AND ARPEGGIO

212. D MINOR (Natural) SCALE AND ARPEGGIO

213. D MINOR (Natural) SCALE AND ARPEGGIO (Lower Octave - Viola and Cello)

214. G MINOR (Natural) SCALE AND ARPEGGIO (Upper Octave - Violin)

215. G MINOR (Natural) SCALE AND ARPEGGIO

216. GREENSLEEVES - Orchestra Arrangement

English Folk Song
Arr. John Higgins

Composition

The process of creating music.

Finish the following example by composing a musical idea.
(Don't forget the title!)

217. _____

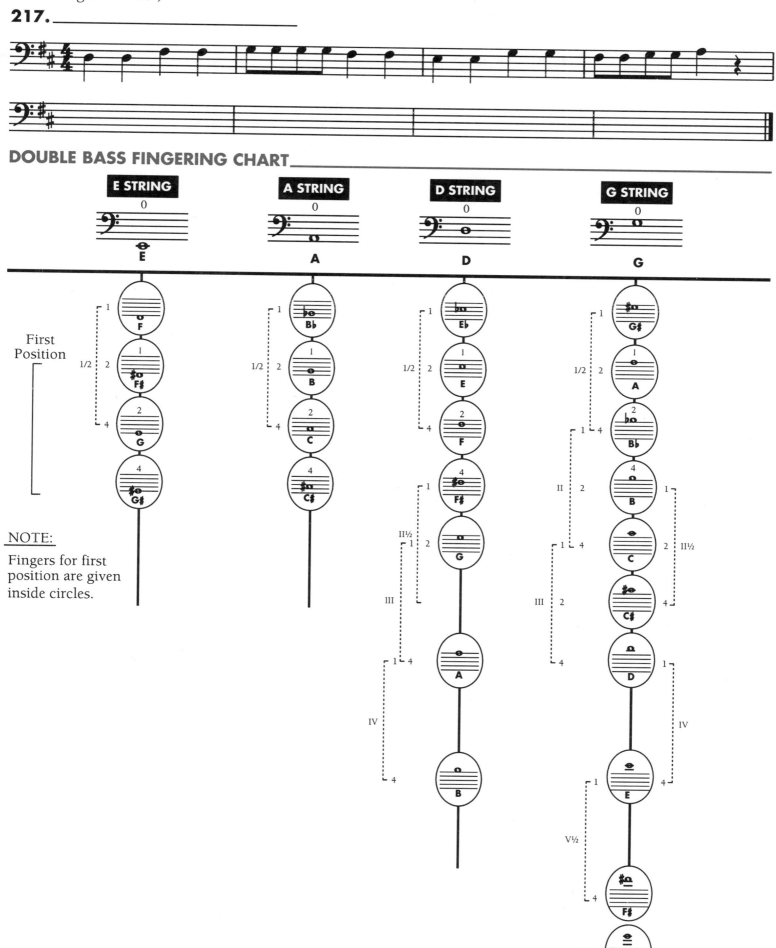

DOUBLE BASS FINGERING CHART

GLOSSARY and INDEX

Essential Element	Definition
A Tempo	Return to original tempo. (p. 19)
Accent	Emphasize the note. (p. 33)
Accidental	Natural, sharp or flat not in key signature. Remains in effect for the full measure.
Allegretto	A lively tempo. (p. 5)
Allegro	Fast bright tempo.
Andante	Slow walking tempo.
Andantino	A tempo that is slightly quicker than *Andante*. (p. 9)
Arco *arco*	Play with the bow on the instrument.
Arpeggio	A chord whose pitches are played one at a time.
Bach, Johann Sebastian	German composer (1685-1750). (p. 24)
Bariolage	A bowing style where no two notes in a row are played on the same string. (p. 41)
Bow Lift	Lift the bow and return to its starting point.
Cantabile	In a singing style. (p. 22)
Cantata	Pieces much like short operas that were written during the Baroque Period (1600-1750). (p. 24)
Carey, Henry	English composer (1689-1743). (p. 33)
Chorale	German hymn or song. (p. 9)
Composition	The process of creating music. (p. 47)
Concerto	A composition in several movements for solo instrument and orchestra. (p. 13)
Crescendo	Gradually increase volume. (p. 3)
Cut Time	Meter in which the half note gets one beat. (p. 36)
D.C. al Fine	Play until D.C. al Fine, go back to beginning, and play until you see Fine.
Decrescendo	Gradually decrease volume. (p. 3)
Dotted Half Note	Three beats of sound.
Dotted Quarter Note	One and one-half beats of sound. (p. 8)
Double Stops	Playing two strings at once. (p. 41)
Down Bow	Move bow away from your body.
e	The Italian word for "and". (p. 10)
Eighth Note	One-half beat of sound.
Eighth Rest	One-half beat of silence. (p. 6)
Fermata	Hold the note longer. (p. 8)
1st and 2nd Endings	Play the 1st ending the 1st time, skip to 2nd ending on repeat.
Flat	Lowers the sound of note(s) a half step.
forte f	Play loudly.
Half Note	Two beats of sound.
Half Rest	Two beats of silence.
Half Step	Smallest distance between two notes.
Harmony	Two or more different pitches sounding at the same time.
Haydn, Franz Joseph	Austrian composer (1732-1809). (p. 9)
Holst, Gustav	British composer (1874-1934). (p. 17)

Essential Element	Definition
Hooked Bowing	Two or more notes played in the same bow direction with a pause in between.
Improvisation	The art of performing music freely, creating your own melody as you play. (p. 41)
Interval	Distance between two notes. (p. 2)
Intonation	How well each note is played in tune. (p. 4)
Key Change	When a key signature changes in the middle of a piece of music. (p. 11)
Legato	Play in a smooth and connected style. (p. 10)
Lento	A very slow tempo. (p. 15)
Mahler, Gustav	German composer (1860-1911). (p. 16)
Major Scale	Series of 8 notes that follow a definite pattern of whole steps and half steps. (p. 2)
Meter Change	A meter (time signature) change in music. (p. 20)
mezzo forte mf	Play moderately loud. (p. 4)
mezzo piano mp	Play moderately soft. (p. 4)
Minor Scale	Series of 8 notes which follow a definite pattern of whole steps and half steps. (p. 16)
Moderato	Moderate tempo.
Natural Sign	Cancels sharps or flats and remains in effect for the full measure.
piano p	Play softly.
Pizzicato *pizz.*	Pluck the strings.
Purcell, Henry	English composer (1659-1695). (p. 29)
Quarter Note	One beat of sound.
Quarter Rest	One beat of silence.
Repeat Sign	Go back to beginning and play the music again.
	Repeat the section of music enclosed by the repeat sign.
Ritardando *(ritard.) (rit.)*	Gradually slow the tempo. (p. 3)
Shadow Bowing	Bowing without the instrument.
Sharp	Raises the sound of note(s) a half step.
Shifting	Sliding your left hand to a new location on the fingerboard.
Sightreading	Playing a musical selection for the first time. (p. 7)
Sixteenth Notes	Four sixteenth notes = One beat of sound. (p. 26)
Slur	Curved line that connects two or more different pitches.
Staccato	Shortened note. Play with stopped bow stroke.
Syncopation	Emphasis on the weak beats of the music. (p. 30)
Tie	Curved line that connects notes of the same pitch.
Triplet	Group of three notes. (p. 40)
Up Bow	Move bow toward your body.
Whole Note	4 beats of sound.
Whole Rest	4 beats of silence.
Whole Step	Two half steps.